Adventurers

HUDSON'S BAY COMPANY ~ THE EPIC STORY

Text by Christopher Moore
Featuring photographs by Kevin Fleming
and images from Hudson's Bay Company's Corporate Art Collection

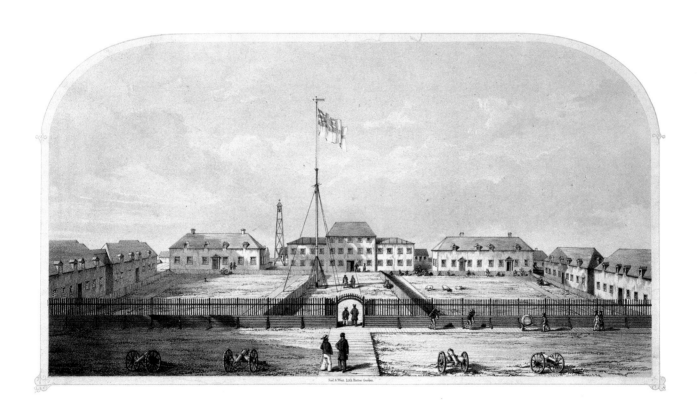

A Quantum Book produced for
HUDSON'S BAY COMPANY

CHAPTER ONE

The Adventurer

1660–1720

Septermber 1668. Four months out from London, the small trading ketch *Nonsuch* noses into the mouth of the Rupert River. By the mast stands a Frenchman who pays no attention to the swirl of English voices around him. Instead he scans the shore with an expert's eye. It is a harsh-looking place, this flat, thinly treed land at the bottom of James Bay. But for Médard Chouart, Sieur des Groseilliers on that September day in 1668, it represents a dream come true.

Seven years before, des Groseilliers, as he is known, and his brother-in-law, Pierre-Esprit Radisson, had travelled to the north of Lake Superior, farther inland than any Frenchmen before them. When winter froze the lakes and streams, they had settled in among their Cree and Ojibwa trading partners to await the spring.

Times were hard, their native hosts told them. Once, traders from the powerful Huron confederacy on the Great Lakes to the south had brought them French kettles, hatchets and blankets and traded for beaver pelts. Then, ten years back, the fall of the Huron nation to its great rival, the Iroquois confederacy, had cut off the northern peoples from the flow of French trade goods. The war still rages, and almost nothing gets through.

Give us another route, the Cree and Ojibwa said. Stay away from the fighting on the Great Lakes.

Des Groseilliers repeated their words when he and Radisson returned to Montreal. If we go by sea to the great salt bay to the north, he explained, we can get around the conflicts to the south. We will trade directly with the hunters of the cold northern regions where the best pelts come from. But New France did not welcome des Groseilliers' plan. Even in wartime,

the fur trade was Montreal's biggest business. The merchants there would never allow it to be diverted to Hudson Bay.

Undaunted, des Groseilliers and Radisson went elsewhere. By 1665 they were in England, and in 1668 des Groseilliers sailed to Hudson Bay.

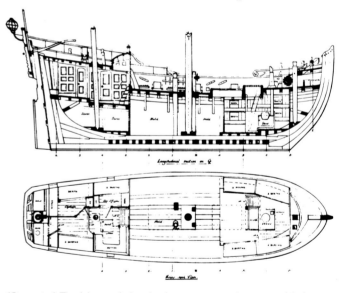

(Opposite) The Nonsuch *battles heavy seas on its way to Hudson Bay. A cramped fifty-three feet (sixteen metres) long, the* Nonsuch *was packed with hundreds of trade goods, including pounds of tobacco and dozens of pairs of shoes, as well as a crew of eleven men.*

The Voyageurs Radisson and des Groseilliers

In France, Médard Chouart's family had owned a piece of land called "des groseilliers," the gooseberry patch. Owning land had prestige, so young Médard added the title "des Groseilliers" to his name. (Much later, Hudson's Bay Company records would list him as "Mister Gooseberry.") He came to New France when he was about twenty-one and lived for a time at Trois-Rivières. But he never settled for long on any patch of land. Instead he spent most of his life travelling, trading, and exploring with his Native allies and friends. He pioneered the *voyageur* way of life in New France — and helped father the North American fur trade.

Pierre Radisson was a recent teenage arrival in New France when he was captured by Iroquois raiders. Several years with them — and suffering torture when he tried to escape — made him a tough, experienced woodsman who spoke several Native languages. Soon after he was freed, his new brother-in-law, des Groseilliers, took him along on the great voyage to the northwest. Later, in England, it was Radisson who took the lead in dealing with the London merchants and investors.

(Above) Radisson and des Groseilliers greet their Native trading partners by the shore of Hudson Bay. (Left) Pierre-Esprit Radisson was the brother-in-law of des Groseilliers.

(Above) It was the beaver and its valuable pelt that drew Radisson and des Groseilliers to Hudson Bay. Many early illustrations of beavers and their ways were done by artists who had never actually seen them. (Left) This 1777 engraving shows beavers living in apartment-style colonies.

At the Rupert River, Captain Zachariah Gillam and his crew beached the *Nonsuch* and built a snug shelter. Des Groseilliers waited with them through a long, cold, quiet winter.

Spring arrived, and Cree traders came down the river. Their canoes rode low in the water, for they were heaped with glossy beaver pelts. They greeted the winterers and exchanged gifts with them. An alliance was struck, and business soon grew brisk. By mid-June, the Cree traders were heading back to their inland homes, their canoes laden with kettles, hatchets, blankets and other goods. The *Nonsuch*, her hold crammed with beaver pelts, set sail for London.

Des Groseilliers was jubilant. Traders living in the snowy encampments of the Canadian north had forged a bond with the great merchant houses of Europe. They had turned the fur trade of North America toward the once almost deserted shores of Hudson Bay.

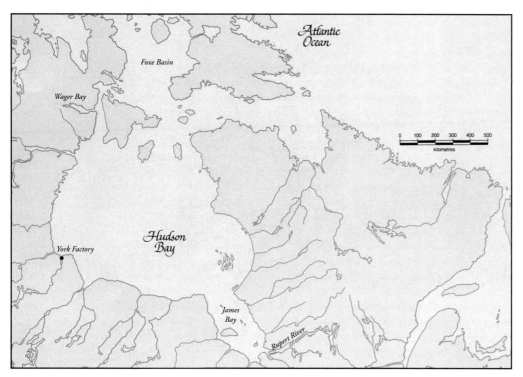

(Top) With a full cargo of furs, the Nonsuch *returned to England in the fall of 1669. Radisson and des Groseilliers had succeeded in establishing a trading route to the rich fur country of the north. Their first winter had been spent near the mouth of the Rupert River (left). In later years, the Company would concentrate its trading at York Factory, at the mouth of the Hayes River on the west side of Hudson Bay.*

"CONTINENTAL"
COCKED HAT.
(1776)

"NAVY"
COCKED HAT.
(1800)

ARMY. (1837)

CLERICAL.
(Eighteenth Century)

(THE WELLINGTON.)
(1812)

CIVIL.

(THE PARIS BEAU.)
(1815)

(THE D'ORSAY.)
(1820)

(THE REGENT.)
(1825)

For Want of a Hat

As odd as it seems, it was a fashion for hats that drew the Company to Hudson Bay.

In the seventeenth century, everyone of style and note wanted a beaver hat. But this was not some furry headgear — when people spoke of a beaver hat, they actually meant one made of felt from the undercoat of the beaver's pelt. Once sheared from the pelt, this fine dense fur, consisting of thousands of short barbed hairs, could be pressed into a glossy felt that was waterproof and could easily be worked into many different styles. Such hats were precious — a man might leave one to his son in his will — and Europe soon developed a thriving used-beaver-hat industry.

The style for beaver hats lasted well into the nineteenth century, when silk overtook it in popularity. By that time, the beaver was prized for its fur, not just its felt.

(Top left) Beaver hats enjoyed a long-lived popularity and came in many styles. (Above) Today, the beaver hat has passed into history. This selection from a costume shop in London, England, is used in historical plays and films.

The English investors who had sent des Groseilliers and the *Nonsuch* to Hudson Bay were powerful people. They included the leading court bankers and the most successful shipowners of London. The King of England himself, Charles II, was interested. These men were not thinking merely of a business in furs. They had seen the East India Company build a trading empire in Asia, and they hoped North America could provide opportunities to match. Once the *Nonsuch*'s voyage proved that a fur trade out of Hudson Bay was practical, des Groseilliers' plan became the inspiration for a great enterprise.

Under the leadership of Prince Rupert, who was an artist, a soldier and a scientist as well as King Charles' "dear and entirely beloved cousin," some of the wealthiest and best-connected men in England pooled their money to found a new company. At Whitehall Palace in London, on May 2, 1670, Charles II of England authorized a Royal Charter that created "The Governor and Company of Adventurers of England tradeing into Hudson's Bay." Thus Hudson's Bay Company, the world's oldest continuing trading company, was born.

Prince Rupert (1619–1682)

The Prince, properly called Prince Rupert of the Rhine, was a nephew of Charles II of England and spent most of his life serving the Stuart kings. He was Charles II's finest cavalry commander, a brilliant admiral, and also an artist, a chemist and a patron of the arts and sciences. Rupert never visited North America, but he gave his name to Rupert's Land, which covered almost half the continent.

King Charles' Charter promised the founders of the new company that they could be "true and absolute Lordes and Proprietors of Rupert's Land" — all the land drained by all the rivers flowing into Hudson Bay. They did not know it yet, but Rupert's Land covered forty percent of modern Canada. Its boundaries stretched from what is now Quebec to Alberta, north into today's Northwest Territories, south into what is now the United States. Within that territory, King Charles authorized the Company to build forts, raise armies, wage wars, found colonies, enforce laws and drive out all competitors. King Charles had created a company with an empire larger than Europe.

(Above) Charles II of England signs the Royal Charter creating the "Company of Adventurers of England tradeing into Hudson's Bay" on May 2, 1670. (Right) Today, the Charter, which features a portrait of the king worked into the letter C in his name, is kept at the Company's head office in Toronto.

The Discoverer of Hudson Bay

Henry Hudson, the man who gave his name to the great bay — and the Company named for it — was a seasoned explorer. Hudson had already made two attempts to find a North West Passage and had journeyed up the Hudson River when he was commissioned by James I of England in 1610 to search for the passage from Europe to China. The lavishly equipped expedition made its way into Ungava Bay and through the treacherous strait that would later bear Hudson's name. Once his ship was again in open water, Hudson mistakenly assumed that he had found the passage — only to be faced with the shorelines of the bay as he headed first east, then west. Trapped in the bay, Hudson and his men spent a miserable winter waiting for their ship to break free of the ice. In June, the sick and hungry sailors mutinied when Hudson refused to give up exploring. They abandoned Captain Hudson, his son and a few loyal sailors, and sailed home to England. Interestingly, while the corporate name is Hudson's Bay Company, the name given on most maps today is Hudson Bay. The letter S was officially dropped early last century.

(Above) Henry Hudson and his loyal crewmen were set adrift by mutinous seamen in the bay that bears his name. (Left) On this seventeenth-century map, Hudson Bay is called Hudsons.

Once the glamour of its founding faded a little, the "Company of Adventurers" set itself to the kind of trading des Groseilliers and the *Nonsuch* had begun at Rupert River in 1668. Soon the Company was sending more ships to Hudson Bay, starting an annual cycle that would last two hundred years.

The Company's men opened trading posts at the mouths of rivers all around Hudson Bay. They put up storehouses. They ran up the Company flag. They built alliances with bands of Cree traders who came to greet them. The pattern for the Company's success was set, although the gentlemen in London would have to wait a few years before they were happily counting any profits.

The Native nations, too, must have been satisfied.

King Charles' men might have a parchment giving them all of Rupert's Land, but the Cree — and their Ojibwa, Montagnais, and Assiniboine allies — knew to whom the land and its trade really belonged. Now they could come down the Rupert River, the Moose River, the Albany River or the Eastmain River to James Bay, or down the Severn River or the Hayes River to the western shore of Hudson Bay. At each place there was a new, permanently occupied Hudson's Bay Company outpost. Kettles, axes and other trade goods began to flow once more to northern peoples who had been cut off from them by the fierce wars on the Great Lakes. Native traders carried the business far into the west, and each spring more canoes came downriver to the Company posts.

Pierre Le Moyne, Sieur d'Iberville (1661–1706)

The son of a prosperous Montreal merchant, Pierre Le Moyne earned a reputation as one of the greatest fighting soldiers and sailors in the history of New France. D'Iberville, to use his title, proved his bravery in 1697 during a battle to capture York Factory. Challenged by a British force of three armed ships, his lone vessel sank one British ship, chased off another and forced a third to surrender. After four hours of fighting, York Factory was his. He went on to fight the English in New York, Acadia, Newfoundland and the West Indies.

and cannons as readily as trade bales. The Company's shareholders were about to learn that New France had woodland fighters as intrepid as its woodland traders.

When des Groseilliers and Radisson went to London, France and England were allies, not enemies. In any case, the two fur traders' true loyalties, it seems, were not to any nation but to the fur trade itself. Gradually they found the Company had not much to offer them. They were veteran woodsmen, eager to take the trade far inland, but the clerks and warehouse keepers the Company sent to Hudson Bay stayed close to their storehouses and stuck to business. Cree traders did the inland travelling and trading. In 1684 des Groseilliers and Radisson went back to New France. Radisson would eventually return to Hudson's Bay Company service, and he died in London about 1710. Des Groseilliers, the founder of an international trading network that connected the woodland traders of northern Canada to the merchant houses of London, died peacefully at home in Trois-Rivières about 1696.

If the Company traders did not give "good measure," however, Cree traders went elsewhere. New France had not abandoned the fur trade when des Groseilliers brought the English to Hudson Bay. The wars with the Iroquois were ending, and Montreal traders were once again venturing westward. They were eager to beat these interlopers from the great bay to the north. To win that battle, they would use muskets

A wigwam belonging to what were called "Home Indians," Cree who lived near Hudson's Bay Company posts and acted as middlemen in the fur trade.

CHAPTER TWO

The Long Struggle with Montreal

1713–1821

York Factory was "nothing but a confused heap of old rotten houses," reported James Knight to the Company's London officers in September 1714. The first Bayman to visit York Factory since the end of the French wars, Knight had come ashore to find that the jewel of the Company trading posts had been reduced to ruins.

From 1686 to 1713, Britain and France had been almost continuously at war. Throughout those years, Pierre de Troyes, Pierre d'Iberville and other fighting soldiers of New France had attacked Hudson's Bay Company's posts by land and sea. They had given New France almost complete control of Hudson Bay. The posts that survived sent few furs to London, and the Company's partners suffered through the "years of no dividend," which lasted twenty-eight years. By the time the war ended, the Company's business had dwindled to something much less than the founders had expected. Now the Company's hopes were reviving.

~

"There is nothing more persistent in the world than these claims of the Hudson's Bay Company," said Britain's envoy to the peace talks with France. The

Company wanted its Hudson Bay trading posts back, and it got them. The Duke of Marlborough, England's greatest general and a former governor of the Company, had helped defeat France's armies on the battlefields of Europe. As part of the price of peace, the French King, Louis XIV, had to hand back the territories and Hudson's Bay Company trading posts which New France had held for twenty years.

The revived company shifted its business west and north, away from its earliest outposts on James Bay. In 1717, James Knight sailed up the west coast of Hudson Bay to open trade with the Chipewyan, a Dene-speaking people who lived north of the Cree territories. At the mouth of the Churchill River, he erected a small trading post. A few years later, the Company would replace it with Fort Prince of Wales, where heavy cannons loomed from stone bastions over the frozen tundra and the icy waters of the Churchill River.

(Opposite) The Duke of Marlborough had been the Company's third governor. His victories as a military commander forced the French to return the Company's posts. (Left) Fort Prince of Wales as it looked and (above) as it is today. Built at the mouth of the Churchill River to protect the Company's lands from the French, the fort surrendered to a French fleet in 1782 before a single shot was fired. The stone fortress, which had taken thirty-eight years to build, was torched and destroyed by the French in half a day. Now only its blackened battlements survive.

Asleep by the Frozen Sea

For most Hudson's Bay Company employees, working at the Company's posts scattered around the great bay was more a test of endurance than heroics. Shipped out from Britain, usually from the north of Scotland, they signed on for periods of up to five years. The spring and summer months were spent trading with the various Natives who arrived at their posts, but it was the long winter, when the great bay filled with ice and the darkness seemed never to end, that the Baymen found hardest to endure. Their sole contact with the outside world came via the once-a-year supply ships, which brought in trade goods and mail and took away the furs and the meticulous accounts the traders kept — written in the dead of winter by flickering candlelight, using ink that had to be thawed for the purpose. Many of those who voyaged to the frozen bay to earn their fortunes never returned, and their graves can be seen at York Factory to this day.

(Above) Coins and paper currency issued by the Company for use at its trading posts. (Left) The cemetery at York Factory. (Below) The main building at York Factory as it looks today.

York Factory stood farther south, on the Hayes River. It had no stone walls, but it was the Company's single most valuable post and it grew into a cluster of some thirty storehouses and barracks. Year after year, it did more business than any other trading post.

York Factory's advantage was its location. The Hayes River provided the traders' best highway to the prime beaver country of the Manitoba lakes and the Saskatchewan River country far to the west. That ensured that York Factory would long remain the gateway to most of Rupert's Land.

Although the Royal Charter of 1670 had granted the Company a vast territory, York Factory and the handful of other trading posts at the edge of the great salt bay were still its only footholds in North America. Baymen rarely visited the interior of Rupert's Land themselves, and their Native customers far inland rarely came down to Hudson Bay or saw the Company's trading posts. Yet every year beaver, marten and muskrat pelts came down to Hudson Bay, while trade goods that came ashore at York Factory travelled far inland.

It was still the Cree and their allied traders who linked the Company with the inland beaver hunters. They had never accepted the Company's claim to own vast territories of northern Canada. This was *their* land, and the beaver trade was their trade.

The Company, in fact, needed only a few dozen employees to manage its trading empire. Most of those came from Scotland's Orkney Islands, the last British stop for Company ships before they put out into the North Atlantic, bound for Hudson Bay. Young Orkneymen did not sign on to be wilderness explorers in the mould of Radisson or des Groseilliers. They expected only to spend several years working or trading at York Factory or Churchill or Moose Factory. In that role, the Company found its Orkney recruits hardy, diligent and loyal.

The Company was getting all the furs that the London market needed, and the shareholders' profits were steady. The governors of the Company were content to let others venture inland, even though some people in Britain complained that the "Company of Adventurers" seemed to be "asleep by the frozen sea."

The Courage of Thanadelthur

Thanadelthur was a Chipewyan, part of the Dene-speaking peoples of the barrenlands north and west of Churchill. About 1713, she staggered, half-starved, into York Factory after escaping from years of captivity among the Cree, her people's traditional enemy. Governor James Knight wanted peace between the hostile Crees and Chipewyans, and Thanadelthur became his ambassador. She convinced the Cree and Chipewyan trading bands to stop fighting each other (below), and the Chipewyans began coming to Fort Prince of Wales to trade. When she fell ill and died in 1717, Governor Knight praised her as a woman "of a very high spirit and of the firmest resolution, and of great courage."

(Above) Birchbark canoes on display at the Canadian Canoe Museum in Peterborough, Ontario. (Right) Voyageurs during a portage. (Below) An illustration of a typical Montreal voyageur.

Montreal's fur traders, meanwhile, were happy to see their rivals staying close to their posts on salt water. The Montreal traders travelled far inland in pursuit of furs, much as des Groseilliers had done long before. The *voyageurs'* hard-driving canoe brigades carried more furs to Montreal than reached all the Baymen's posts combined. By the 1740s, soldier and explorer Pierre de La Vérendrye had built French forts almost within sight of the Rocky Mountains.

In 1763, after James Wolfe had captured Quebec City, France ceded most of its North American domains to Britain. The Company's governors hoped at first that the end of French rule might put an end to Montreal's annoying rivalry in the competition for furs. Instead, as British businessmen settled in Montreal, the city's fur enterprises become better financed, better organized, and much larger than ever.

The *voyageurs* pushed farther inland, coming ever closer to the Company's trading routes. The Baymen found themselves in a life-or-death competition with Montreal's North West Company, which threatened to choke off the supply of pelts to the bayside trading posts.

In 1774, after a hundred years by Hudson Bay, the Company made a dramatic decision. The governors decided they must go head-to-head with the "Nor'Westers." That year Samuel Hearne built Cumberland House, far upriver from York Factory in what is now northern Saskatchewan. A forty-year battle — the Baymen versus Montreal for control of the fur trade — had begun.

Samuel Hearne (1745–1792)

In 1769, stories of copper deposits far to the northwest reached Fort Prince of Wales. Samuel Hearne, a newcomer to Hudson Bay but already an enthusiastic snowshoe traveller, set out with native guides, moving slowly and following the migrating caribou. It was "all feasting or all famine," Hearne said. After terrible hardships, the travellers reached the Coppermine River and got safely back. Hearne went inland again in 1774 to build the first inland Hudson's Bay Company trading post at Cumberland House, in what is now Saskatchewan. The Company never found any copper mines, but Hearne's book, *A Voyage from Prince of Wales's Fort*, is a Canadian adventure classic.

(Top) The crest of the North West Company.
(Left) Samuel Hearne carved his name in the rock near Churchill, Manitoba.

A Diet of Pemmican

Because the *voyageurs* travelled light and fast, they couldn't carry much food, and they didn't have time to hunt for it along the way. Instead, in this era before refrigeration, they depended on pemmican. Said to taste like cold beef mixed with rancid fat and hair, pemmican was made of buffalo meat cut into strips, and then left to dry on a rack (right) or over a fire. The strips were pounded into a pulp, then placed in a rawhide sack made from the buffalo's hide — along with copious amounts of boiling buffalo fat and saskatoon berries, which helped prevent scurvy. On a typical trip, a *voyageur* would consume about a pound and a half of pemmican a day. It could be eaten as it was, made into soup, or covered with flour and then fried. Pemmican never seemed to

go bad, no matter how long the trip. Indeed, there are reports of people eating pemmican that had been prepared more than fifty years before — without any apparent ill effects.

From 1774 to 1820, Baymen and Nor'Westers waged a desperate struggle for furs. Each side built dozens of trading posts. Rival posts confronted each other at portages and river mouths throughout Rupert's Land. Together the rival companies pushed the trade farther west and farther north. Nor'Wester Peter Pond reached the Athabaska lakes in 1778. Alexander Mackenzie, another Nor'Wester, travelled to the Arctic in 1789, and he pushed over the mountains and all the way to the Pacific Ocean in 1793. David Thompson, a Bayman gone over to the Nor'Westers, mapped much of western Canada as he opened new trading territories. At every step, new alliances drew new tribal groups into the trade.

Beaver were being trapped out in broad stretches of the fur trade territory, but the relentless race westward brought pelts in ever-increasing numbers down to Montreal and Hudson Bay. When Lord Selkirk, a Hudson's Bay Company investor, sent Scottish settlers to Red River, right on the North West Company's route to Montreal, the Nor'Westers reacted furiously. At Seven Oaks, Selkirk's governor, Robert Semple, and twenty settlers were gunned down by allies of the Nor'Westers.

There were too many forts and too many clerks, buying too many pelts just to keep the other side from getting them. Both sides were going broke. Finally, in 1821, the Baymen and the Nor'Westers reached a truce. The Nor'Westers had won most of the battles — their explorers had consistently gone farther and fought harder — but the Company had deeper pockets and more friends in the British government. It won the war. The arrangement they made was called an "amalgamation," but one of the Nor'Westers said, "This is not amalgamation, it is submersion." In a few years, Montreal's two-hundred-year-old fur trade was winding down. At last the company Prince Rupert had founded, truly ruled the trade of Rupert's Land.

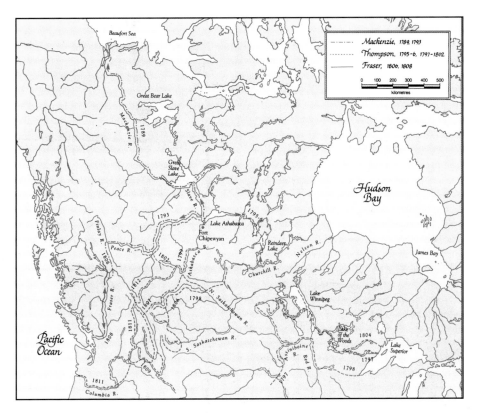

(Opposite) On June 19, 1816, the competition between the Baymen and the Nor'Westers turned violent. At Seven Oaks, Robert Semple and twenty of the settlers sent by Lord Selkirk to establish a Red River colony were gunned down by Nor'Westers enraged that their settlement blocked the canoe route to Montreal. (Above) Lord Selkirk. (Left) Prompted by their competition with the Baymen, Nor'Westers such as Mackenzie, Thompson and Simon Fraser pushed ever farther north and west, searching for new territories.

Give Us Good Measure

1821–1870

*I*t sounds like . . . music. How can that be? Everyone rushes to the gate of the lonely trading post that dozes in the warmth of a summer afternoon at the head of a lake in the heart of Rupert's Land.

Around the point, two canoes come racing, flying across the water at a killing pace. Nine paddlers in matching dress, singing at the top of their lungs, bring the larger one surging up to the dock. They fall silent, and from the canoe a bagpiper leaps ashore. Behind him strides a man robed in a magnificent tartan cloak with a tall beaver hat on his head.

George Simpson, the master of Rupert's Land, has arrived. He prowls rapidly about the post. He inspects the stores. He leafs through the accounts. He interrogates the chief trader, but he does not smile. This post is slack and sloppy, he soon concludes. Too few furs coming in, too much given in exchange. He thinks he will close the place.

Simpson has barely arrived, but already he is ordering his paddlers back to the canoes. They have come seventy-five miles since two o'clock this morning, he explains curtly. He wants to make it a hundred before they stop for the night. Simpson and his elite paddling team had left York Factory just thirty-five days ago, and he intends to be on the Pacific within a month.

In moments, the two canoes have vanished upriver. Only the echo of the paddlers' song remains to convince the bewildered men that the governor's inspection really happened.

~

As far back as the elders could remember, the people had traded beaver pelts for clothing, flour, tools and guns that came from far away. Once they had traded with the Cree who lived downriver and travelled back and forth. Later, Company men and Montrealers had come themselves to build trading posts not far away.

(Left) A formal portrait of George Simpson, appointed governor of the Company in 1821. (Opposite) Simpson travelled up to one hundred miles a day during his speedy tours of the Company's trading posts.

Trading Pelts for Goods

The Company had come to the shores of Hudson Bay looking for beaver, and beaver pelts soon became the standard measure for doing business. Pelts could be exchanged for such items as guns, pots, copper wire and steel traps. Prices were quoted in numbers of "made" beaver (good-quality pelts from an adult beaver). Other furs were accepted, of course, but beaver was the standard — two otter skins were worth only one beaver pelt, but one moose skin was worth two. The famous Hudson's Bay blanket, which the Company introduced in the late eighteenth century, was worth six beaver pelts. This was indicated by the short black stripes along one of its edges — which still appear on the blankets today. But the blanket was for more than sleeping. Often they were used for clothing such as leggings and mittens. Sometimes they were rigged up as temporary shelters and even used as sails on York boats.

(Above) Natives at a Company trading post. (Right) A selection of the goods the Company offered, including pots, rifles and the ever-popular Hudson's Bay blanket.

THE TRADING-STORE.

It was never just business. Just as the beaver and other animals were their friends and providers, the visiting traders were friends and allies. The people and the traders had always exchanged gifts before they exchanged goods. "Give us good measure," the people said. If the traders were not generous, or if their trade goods were not what the people wanted, there were other traders. Montrealer or Bayman, each wanted the people's beaver pelts so much that they had come into the country to ask for them, and they competed to give the best price.

Now there was only the Company, and the people found their partner growing less generous. The Company's new governor closed the nearest posts, so that the people had to carry their pelts greater distances. The Company told the people what furs to bring, and how many were wanted, and the trading posts offered less in exchange for them. It was as if the people were

no longer partners in the trade. Their old ally was acting like a master.

The Company had always been more interested in shipping beaver pelts than wielding the imperial authority its Charter had granted to it. From the 1670s to the 1820s, it had had to work hard to win the business of its Native partners and to withstand the relentless competition from Montreal.

After 1821, the Company's control of the fur trade really did extend across Rupert's Land, and also north to the Arctic Sea and west to the Pacific. Across that vast territory, the Company had become the only buyer of pelts, the only supplier of trade goods. The Baymen were becoming what King Charles' Charter had called them long before: "true and absolute Lordes and Proprietors." The Company could no longer simply stick to trade. It was a government now, too.

Business still came first. After the merger with the NorthWest Company, the London governors intended to take control back from tough explorers and backwoods traders. They sent young George Simpson to put an end to waste. Simpson knew nothing of furs at first, but he learned quickly. He soon took charge of the Company's Canadian empire.

George Simpson's aim was to keep everything the Baymen did, even at the most remote trading posts, under the thumb of the London governors. To put his stamp on every outpost of the Company, he travelled relentlessly back and forth across the continent year after year, ruthlessly imposing his ideas and dismissing anyone who displeased him. "Worn-out traders are the most useless helpless class of men," he said coldly, "and the sooner the Company can get rid of them after their days of activity and labour are over, the better."

In the name of efficiency and profit, George Simpson closed down trading posts. He made sure that ships and riverboats replaced canoes wherever possible. He dismissed hundreds of employees and demanded absolute obedience from those left. He controlled how much fur the Company would buy, and he slashed the prices it would pay.

Simpson wanted to control the Company's Native trading partners, too. He swore he would rule the Native trappers and traders with "a rod of iron." He wanted them in "a proper state of subordination" to the Company. For the first time, the Native nations

York Boats

Named York boats because their most common destination was York Factory, these sturdy double-ended vessels began replacing canoes in the early nineteenth century. Although they weren't fast, and they had to be rolled along on logs during portages, York boats could carry three times the cargo of freight canoes. Throughout the nineteenth century, the Company sent vast fleets, called brigades, to York Factory each year. As pioneers flooded the west, York boats began to carry more general cargo — including pianos and cathedral bells. The last one was built for the Company in 1924.

had no one else to sell to or buy from. They began to lose their share of control of a fur trade that had always needed them. Epidemics that had followed the fur traders in their wild race across the continent thinned their numbers, and they gradually became dependent on Hudson's Bay Company posts in ways they had never been before.

Under Simpson's leadership, fur trading grew very profitable for the Company. But the Company was also governing an empire, and government seemed an endless headache for it.

On the Pacific coast, the Company ran a business that had changed greatly from the days when birchbark canoes paddled up and down the rivers from Hudson Bay. Here supplies from London arrived in ships that travelled around Cape Horn at the tip of South America. Even the inland shipments were carried by horse brigades, not canoes. By the 1830s, the Company had its own steamship, the *Beaver*, plying the inland passages of the west coast.

(Above) The *Beaver*, a paddle-wheel steamer used for trading along the Pacific coast, visited small isolated inlets where sailing ships could not venture. She ran aground off Vancouver in 1888.

But settlement threatened the fur traders' world. American settlers flooded into the Oregon Territory. In 1843, the Company moved north to Fort Victoria on Vancouver Island, but farmers, fishers, loggers, traders, coal miners and gold seekers quickly settled in around the fur trade posts and routes. In the 1850s, James Douglas, the Company's chief factor on the coast, became Great Britain's governor of the fast-growing colonies of Vancouver Island and British Columbia. On the coast, the limitless Hudson's Bay Company trade monopoly faded away, until it was just one more business in a busy community.

The Company faced similar challenges in the heart of Rupert's Land. Around Red River, Métis hunters and farmers, English "half-breeds," and

(Left) Sir James Douglas. Shown here dressed as the British colonial governor on the west coast, he originally had been the Company's chief factor in the region.

John Rae and the Franklin Expedition

John Rae was trained as a doctor but made his name as an explorer. In 1833, the Company sent him to Moose Factory as the resident physician. But the young surgeon soon established himself as the most skillful Arctic explorer of his time, one of the few who learned from the Inuit and employed their methods. Rae was also instrumental in helping to solve one of the great mysteries of his time. In 1845, two ships had left England under the command of Sir John Franklin to find the North West Passage. The ships never returned, and search parties sent to look for the expedition found nothing. In 1854, Rae met an Inuk wearing the gold braid from a naval officer's cap. He told Rae of a group of white men who had died far away. During subsequent meetings, other Inuit gave Rae more objects, including a plate with Franklin's name on it. From what they told him, Rae concluded that Franklin's ships had been crushed in the ice, and the crews had abandoned them. They had then starved to death before they could reach safety.

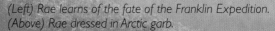
(Left) Rae learns of the fate of the Franklin Expedition.
(Above) Rae dressed in Arctic garb.

(Above) Lower Fort Garry was among the Company's most important posts by the middle of the nineteenth century. The city of Winnipeg grew up around it. (Left) This muskox skull, used as a towel rack, still hangs in the Men's House — the home for the unmarried men — at Lower Fort Garry today.

Lord Selkirk's Scots settlers had built a lively, thriving community. They wanted freedom of trade and they wanted control of their own destiny. Even many who worked for the Company were unwilling to have it continue to act as their government as well. In the 1840s, Métis leaders asked Britain to do away with the Company's claim to Rupert's Land. The country around Red River was Métis land, they said. The Company should own nothing but a few trading posts.

By the 1860s, the Company faced a challenge from Canada, too. The farmers of Canada West — what is now Ontario — yearned to move onto the fertile western prairie. Once Confederation was achieved in 1867, Canada was eager to expand its boundaries westward. George Brown, one of the Fathers of Canadian Confederation, wanted to abolish what he called "the injurious and demoralizing sway of the Hudson's Bay Company."

In 1869, almost two hundred years after it received its great Charter, the Company sat at the bargaining table with the British and Canadian governments and bartered away its monopoly of trade and its vast territorial domain in North America. The Company became what some of its shareholders had always wanted it to be: a simple commercial enterprise.

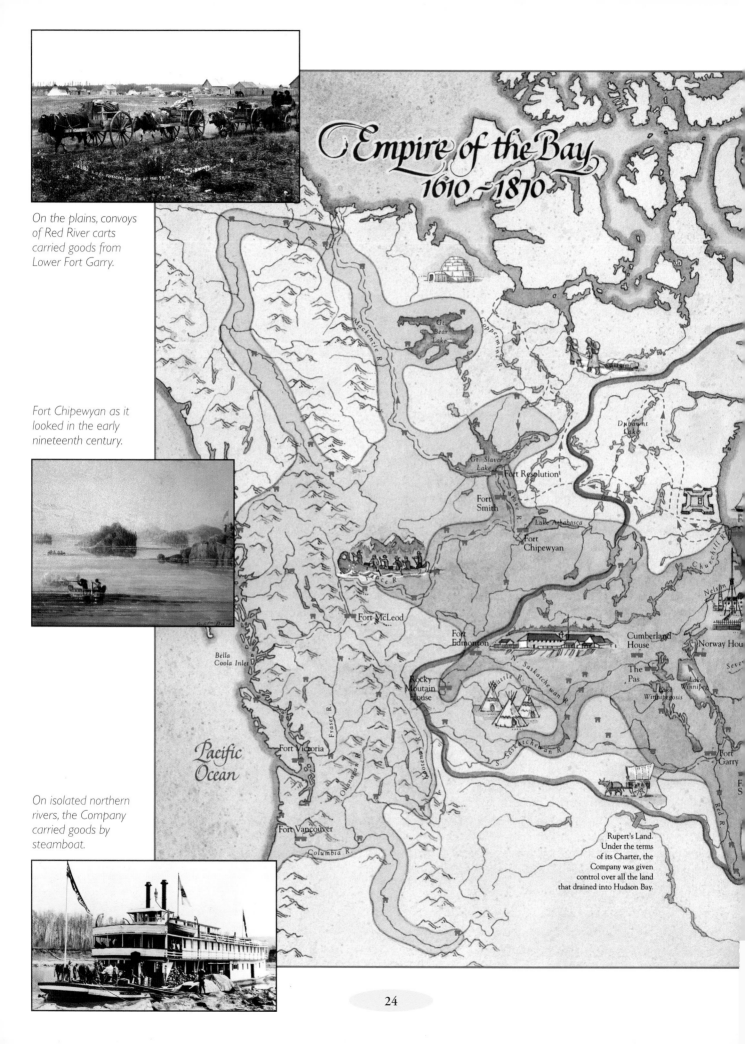

On the plains, convoys of Red River carts carried goods from Lower Fort Garry.

Fort Chipewyan as it looked in the early nineteenth century.

On isolated northern rivers, the Company carried goods by steamboat.

Empire of the Bay 1610~1870

Gt. Bear Lake

Mackenzie R.

Coppermine R.

Dubawnt Lake

Gt. Slave Lake

Fort Resolution

Fort Smith

Slave R.

Lake Athabasca

Fort Chipewyan

Churchill R.

Nelson R.

Peace R.

Fort McLeod

Fort Edmonton

N. Saskatchewan R.

Cumberland House

Norway House

The Pas

Lake Winnipegosis

Lake Winnipeg

Sever

Bella Coola Inlet

Rocky Moutain House

Battle R.

S. Saskatchewan R.

Fort Garry

Pacific Ocean

Fraser R.

Kootenay R.

Okanagan R.

Fort Victoria

Red R.

Fort Vancouver

Columbia R.

Rupert's Land. Under the terms of its Charter, the Company was given control over all the land that drained into Hudson Bay.

24

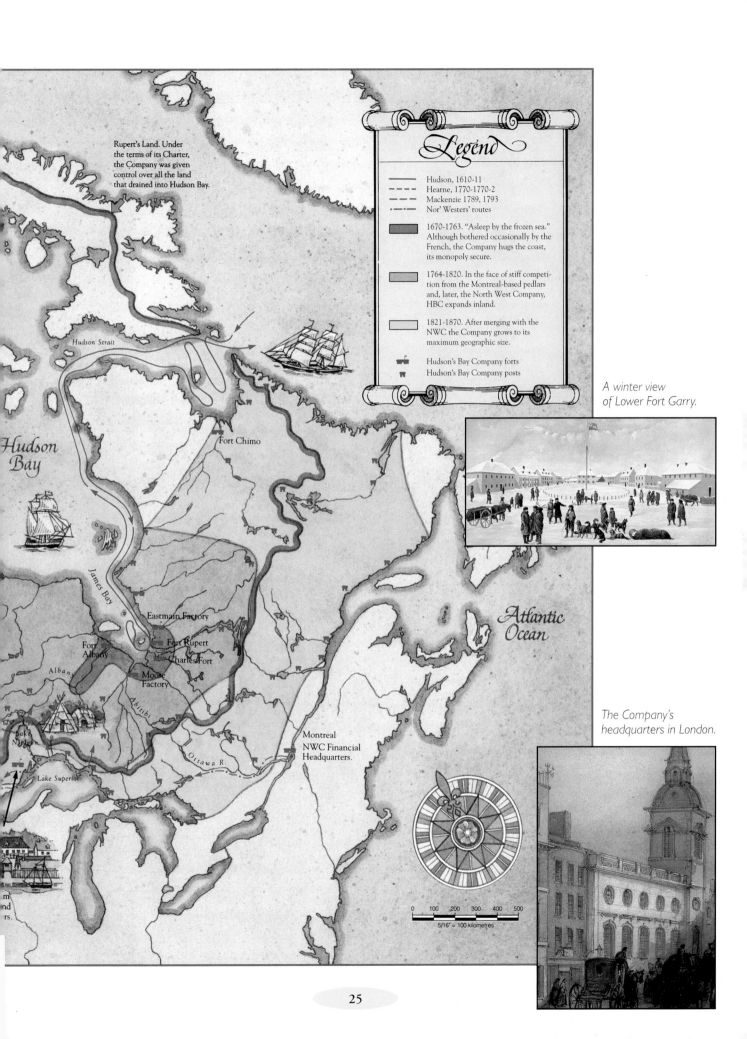

Rupert's Land. Under the terms of its Charter, the Company was given control over all the land that drained into Hudson Bay.

Hudson Strait

Hudson Bay

Fort Chimo

James Bay

Eastmain Factory

Fort Albany

Fort Rupert

Charles Fort

Moose Factory

Albany

Abitibi

Lake Nipissing

Lake Superior

Ottawa R.

Montreal
NWC Financial Headquarters.

Atlantic Ocean

A winter view of Lower Fort Garry.

The Company's headquarters in London.

0   100   200   300   400   500

5/16" = 100 kilometres

CHAPTER FOUR

Becoming A Business

1870–2000

August 1881. Winnipeg, Manitoba. With construction of the transcontinental railway moving rapidly ahead, Winnipeg has become the boom town of the west. Now something almost as big and exciting as the CPR has opened at Main and York. The company that had built a trading post called Fort Garry long before anyone dreamed of a city called Winnipeg has now opened a Hudson's Bay Company department store three storeys high and a full city block long.

Excited Winnipeggers wander through it, fingering sensible English woollens, examining the hunting rifles, and trying on the snowshoe costumes. They gaze in wonder at stacks of Russian caviar, displays of Belgian lace, and fine musical instruments. The Hudson's Bay Company name means more than beaver now!

When the Company gave up its territorial empire in 1870, furs for fashion were replacing pelts for hatmaking. But it continued to run a thriving business in furs. HBC headquarters at Beaver House in London could proudly claim to be one of the great centres of the worldwide fur trade, and the Company's fur auction business was among the world's largest. With settlement spreading across Canada, the fur business moved farther into the north, and the Company went with it, exporting furs and importing supplies the way it always had. For most of the twentieth century, a Hudson's Bay Company trading post, along with an RCMP detachment and a Christian mission, stood at the heart of many northern communities. Hudson's Bay factors were doctors, diplomats and radio operators as well as shopkeepers.

Donald Smith (1820–1914)

Smith spent decades as a Hudson's Bay Company fur trader in remote Labrador and eventually became governor of the Company. The wealth he amassed serving the Company enabled him to invest in the Canadian Pacific Railway. As one of its principal shareholders, the old fur trader had the honour of hammering in the last spike for the transcontinental railway in 1885. In 1897, Queen Victoria made him Lord Strathcona.

(Left) The first modern Hudson's Bay Company department store. Its displays were more lavish than anyone in Winnipeg had ever seen before, as shown in this photograph (above) from the 1890s.

In this 1940s photograph, a Hudson's Bay Company storekeeper and an Inuit trapper barter fox furs for goods. Notice that even the employee is wearing a fur jacket. The Company's posts in the north were often unheated to discourage customers from lingering around a warm store instead of tending their trap lines.

Transporting Company Goods in the Twentieth Century

As the nineteenth century gave way to the twentieth, new means of transportation replaced the traditional canoes and York boats. In cities where the Company was building its new stores, delivery wagons were used, then trucks not long before the First World War. To bring in supplies to the north and serve its increasingly scattered posts, the Company had its own fleet of cargo ships. Most famous of these was the tough *Nascopie*, designed to punch her way through the ice. Built in 1912, she also served on convoys during the First World War and even chased off an attack by a German submarine. For more than three decades, the *Nascopie* headed north from Montreal each spring and into Hudson Bay, visiting countless small posts to land supplies and take away furs. In 1947, she hit an uncharted reef and sank.

In the 1930s, the Company also started to use small airplanes to keep its distant posts supplied. Journeys that had once taken days by canoe or York boat could now be made in hours.

(Left) The Nascopie *makes its way through heavy ice. (Below) Early airplanes such as this were used increasingly to carry goods during the 1930s. (Bottom) A Winnipeg HBC delivery truck from 1912.*

For people who lived far from its modern stores, a Hudson's Bay Company mail-order catalogue was created. (Left) These illustrations of women's fashions from an early catalogue would have matched anything found in the ladies' department of the Company's stores (above).

From 1670 to 1870, the Company had never entirely occupied the vast territory King Charles' Charter had 'granted' to it. Still, when it gave up its claims to Rupert's Land in 1870, the Company received about seven million acres (2.8 million hectares) of land in compensation. These acres soon became very valuable, for immigrants hungry for land were coming to settle the prairie west. At the start of the twentieth century, HBC's Land Department, established to sell what remained of King Charles' land grant, was the Company's most flourishing enterprise.

Later, it grew into an important land developer, building office complexes and shopping centres in cities across Canada. It also invested in Canadian resource industries, and Hudson's Bay Oil and Gas Company became one of the Company's most important investments for much of the twentieth century.

From Sea to Sea

For more than 200 years, Hudson's Bay Company was very much a western and northern concern. Only in the early years of the twentieth century did this begin to change. In the 1920s, the Company moved east, into Canada's maritime provinces, becoming involved in Prince Edward Island's booming silver fox industry. Later, it became active in the Newfoundland fishery, packing salmon for sale in its stores under the Hubay and Labdor labels (below).

(Left) For over fifty years the Company was heavily involved in the oil and gas industry. Here a Company-owned well pumps crude oil in western Canada.

Mostly, however, the Company became the store-keeper to the nation. The department store it opened in Winnipeg in 1881 became the first of many. In Vancouver, the first Hudson's Bay store opened barely a year after the city was incorporated in 1886. Early in the twentieth century, Company directors Leonard Cunliffe and Sir Richard Burbidge, using department-store expertise they had gained at the famed Harrod's of London, helped the Company build up the largest retailing enterprise in Canada. Right across the country, "The Bay" (as it called its stores after 1965) opened handsome department stores on downtown main streets and in new suburban shopping centres. Starting with Morgans of Montreal in 1960, the Company absorbed or replaced several distinguished names in Canadian retailing, including Woodward's, Freiman's, Simpson's, and Zellers.

Between 1960 and 1999 the Company expanded its reach by acquiring stores all across Canada. Among these were Morgans, a Montreal retailer since Victorian times (left), and Simpson's, whose flagship Toronto store (above) had long been a city landmark.

Soapstone Sculptures

Evocative Inuit soapstone carvings are a symbol of Canada throughout the world. In 1949, a Baffin Island-based Bayman named Norman Ross helped gather together samples of the work done by local Inuit carvers to send south. Interest was strong, and a booming market for Inuit carvings and, later on, prints evolved. For many years, Hudson's Bay Company was the largest purchaser of these, buying as much as forty tons of soapstone sculpture for resale in a single year.

Western Canada's Woodward's stores (below) were also absorbed into HBC's retail operation. (Left) Zellers, acquired in 1978, is today Canada's largest mass merchandise department store chain.

In 1970, on its three-hundredth anniversary, Hudson's Bay Company headquarters moved from London to Canada. Today, the handsome decorated parchment and wax seal that is the Royal Proclamation Charter of May 2, 1670, can be seen in Canada. Sealed under protective glass, it has a proud place in the Company's Toronto offices.

The modern Hudson's Bay Company, however, has left the fur trade which created it and which it influenced so greatly. In 1987, the Company sold its fur department and northern stores division. Across the land once called Rupert's Land, the fur trade endures. Hunters and trappers still look to the land as their ancestors did, and still go out in the cold and snow to harvest pelts.

Today's Hudson's Bay Company

The Company's final acquisition of the twentieth century was seventeen Eaton's locations. Added to the over five hundred Bay, Zellers, and Fields stores, the acquisition contributed to HBC's status as the largest department store retailer in Canada and the country's fifth-largest corporation. As the twenty-first century dawned, Hudson's Bay Company employees numbered 70,000 people and the Company's annual revenues exceeded seven billion dollars. New investments were being made in the realm of electronics and e-commerce. At the world's oldest chartered company, business continues.

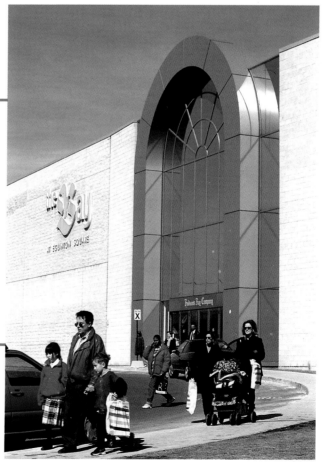

(Left) George Heller, Company president and C.E.O. in 2000, began his career with HBC at a trading post in Winisk (now Peawanuck), Ontario. (Right) A Bay store today.

Index

Text © 2000 Christopher Moore and Hudson's Bay Company
Photographs, design and compilation © 2000 Hudson's Bay Company

Canadian Cataloguing in Publication Data

Moore, Christopher
    Adventurers: Hudson's Bay Company — The Epic Story

A Quantum book produced for Hudson's Bay Company.
Includes index.
ISBN 1-895892-13-9

1. Hudson's Bay Company — History — Juvenile literature.
2. Northwest, Canadian — Juvenile literature. 3. Fur trade — Canada - History — Juvenile literature. I. Hudson's Bay Company. II. Title.

FC3207.M66 2000   j971.2'01   C00-931988-3
F1060.35.M66 2000

Produced by Madison Press Books for The Quantum Book Group Inc.
149 Lowther Avenue, Toronto, Ontario, Canada M5R 3M5

Printed in Hong Kong

Design and Page Composition

Joseph Gisini / PageWave Graphics Inc.

Picture Credits

Canadian Canoe Museum: 14 (top)

Kevin Fleming: 6 (right), 7 (bottom left), 11 (top), 12 (all), 15 (bottom left), 20 (right), 23 (bottom), back cover (top)

Hudson's Bay Company Corporate Collection: front cover, 4 (top right), 5 (top), 7 (top), 7 (bottom right; photo by Kevin Fleming), 8 (right), 10, 11 (bottom), 18, 22 (bottom left), 23 (top), 26, 29 (bottom left), 30 (all), 31 (all)

Hudson's Bay Company Archives/Provincial Archives of Manitoba: 1, 2, 3, 4 (bottom right and left), 8 (left), 9 (bottom), 13, 15 (bottom right), 19, 20 (left), 21 (bottom), 24 (middle), 24 (bottom), 25 (all), 27 (all), 28 (bottom left, middle and right), 29 (bottom right), 29 (top left and right), back cover (left)

Maps by Jack McMaster: 5 (bottom), 17 (bottom), 24-25

National Archives of Canada: 4 (top left), 6 (left), 9 (top), 14 (middle), 14 (bottom), 15 (top right), 16 (all), 28 (top), back cover (bottom right)

Provincial Archives of Alberta: 24 (top)

Provincial Archives of Ontario: 21 (top)

Provincial Archives of British Columbia: 22 (top left)

Glenbow Museum: 22 (right)

Toronto Public Library: 17 (top)